SCIENCE IN SECONDS AT THE BEACH

with Activities for Ponds, Lakes, and Rivers

Exciting Experiments You Can Do in Ten Minutes or Less

Jean Potter

JOHN WILEY & SONS, INC.

New York • Chichester • Weinheim • Brisbane • Singapore • Toronto

This book is dedicated to my dearest little friend,
Schuyler Eden Mizikar Harvath,
who shares all the goodness, love, and joys of childhood with us.
You have changed our lives, dear one.

Special thanks to:
Thomas, my husband, for his love and encouragement
Archie, our Welsh corgi, for his companionship
Shadow, our Russian blue, for his entertainment
Mom, Dad, Kathy, Emmett, Charley, my family, for so much
Kate Bradford, my editor, for her faith, advice, and constructive criticism

This text is printed on acid-free paper. ⧝

Copyright © 1998 by Jean Potter
Illustrations © 1998 by Tina Cash Walsh

Published by John Wiley & Sons, Inc.
All rights reserved. Published simultaneously in Canada.

The publisher and the author have made every reasonable effort to ensure that the experiments and activities in this book are safe when conducted as instructed but assume no responsibility for any damage caused or sustained while performing the experiments or activities in the book. Parents, guardians, and/or teachers should supervise young readers who undertake the experiments and activities in this book.

Library of Congress Cataloging-in-Publication Data

Potter, Jean.
    Science in seconds at the beach : exciting experiments you can do in
10 minutes or less / Jean Potter.
        p.   cm.
    Includes index.
    Summary: Presents a variety of experiments that investigate
scientific disciplines, including biology, geology, weather,
physics, and more and can be done at a beach, swimming pool, or even
in the bathtub.
    ISBN 0-471-17899-3 (pbk. : alk. paper)
    1. Science—Experiments—Juvenile literature.   2. Beaches—Study
and teaching (Elementary)—Juvenile literature.   [1. Science—
Experiments.   2. Experiments.]   I. Title.
Q164.P76   1998
507'.8—dc21   97-39799

10 9 8 7 6 5 4 3 2 1

Contents

Sand and Rocks   57

Shells   69

Sun   81

Water   91

Water Movement   101

Introduction

Science in Seconds at the Beach contains over 100 quick and easy experiments that will help you investigate the mysteries of animals, plants, sand, shells, sun, and water. Each activity takes only ten minutes or less to set up and finish, even though a few experiments need to be "read" after a certain amount of time has passed. While most activities take place at or near the beach, some can be done in a kitchen, swimming pool, or bathtub.

HOW THIS BOOK IS ORGANIZED

Science in Seconds at the Beach is divided into sections by topic. Each experiment answers a particular question about science and includes a list of the materials you need, easy-to-follow steps, and an explanation of what the experiment demonstrates. You may want to visit the library or an aquarium for additional information on the topic.

TIPS FOR COMPLETING THE EXPERIMENTS

When conducting experiments, follow the directions closely. These tips will help:

Be Prepared. Is the beach you will visit at an ocean, lake, or pond? Is the water salty or fresh? Is the beach sandy or rocky? Look up possible experiments ahead of time and make a list of materials to pack. Take along boots for rocky beaches and sneakers for beaches with shells. Do not wander alone on the beach or anywhere else—take a friend along. Pack a pair of thongs or old sneakers to protect your feet while wading. Dress to get wet! Before beginning any experiment, assemble all the materials in the order you will use them.

Be Careful. Use caution when climbing on slippery rocks. Never go into the water without an adult watching you. Remember that the beach is home to many tiny animals, so watch where you step.

Be Considerate. Always leave the beach cleaner than you found it. Pick up any mess you make, as well as trash that was left by others. Put waste in the proper containers. Fill in any holes you dig. Handle living plants and small beach animals with care, and always put animals back where you found them.

ANIMALS

Animals are living creatures with the power of **locomotion** (movement). Hundreds of thousands of different kinds of animals live on Earth, and more kinds are still being discovered.

In this section you will learn amazing facts about some animals that live at the beach or in the water, including a very unusual bird, crabs that live in snail shells, and creatures that live in seaweed.

BIRD PADDLE

How Are the Feet of Swimming Birds Different from Those of Nonswimming Birds?

MATERIALS

ocean, lake, or pond beach
binoculars
adult helper

PROCEDURE

1. Sit quietly on the beach, watching for birds walking on the shore.
2. Use the binoculars to look at the birds' feet. What do you notice about their toes?
3. Have an adult watch as you wade into the water. Spread your fingers wide and move your hands through the water.
4. Put your fingers together on each hand and move your hands through the water. What's different from when you had your fingers spread?

EXPLANATION

You noticed that swimming birds have **webbed feet** (feet on which the toes are connected by skin). Webbed feet work like paddles, helping the bird push through the water. When you spread your fingers apart in the water, you could not push very well through the water. When you put your fingers together, you could push better through the water.

OILY FEATHERS

How Does Oil Spilled into Water Affect Swimming Birds?

MATERIALS

2 bowls of water
paper towels
eyedropper
vegetable oil
2 feathers

PROCEDURE

1. Set the bowls of water next to each other on a flat surface and spread paper towels around the bowls.
2. Use the eyedropper to drop a few drops of vegetable oil on the water in one bowl.
3. Dip one feather in the plain water, then pull the feather out and wave it in the air above the paper towels. Examine the feather.
4. Dip the other feather in the oily water, then pull the feather out and wave it in the air over the paper towels. Examine the feather. What differences can you see between the feathers?
5. Use the paper towels for cleanup.

EXPLANATION

The water slid off the feather that was dipped in the plain water, and the feather appeared dry. The feather that was dipped in the oily water soaked up the oil and became heavier. When a bird swims in an **oil slick** (area of oil floating on water), its feathers soak up the oil and the bird can't fly. If the bird can't fly, it won't be able to find food and will eventually starve to death.

SHELL PILES

What Causes Piles of Shells on the Ocean Beach?

MATERIALS

ocean beach

PROCEDURE

1. Walk up and down the beach late in the afternoon, looking for piles of shells.

2. When you find a pile, examine the sand around the pile. What do you see?

EXPLANATION

If you saw holes and bird prints in the sand, the shell pile was the garbage from a bird's meal. An **oystercatcher** is a chicken-size beach bird with a blackish-brown-and-white body, long red bill, and pink feet. The oystercatcher pokes its powerful beak into the sand to find **bivalves** (ocean animals that form shells with two halves, such as oysters and scallops). The oystercatcher uses its beak to hammer open the shell and pick out the animal. An oystercatcher can eat as many as 400 bivalves in one day.

6

WALKING SHELLS

How Can Animals with Shells Walk?

MATERIALS

book with pictures of lobsters, shrimps, prawns, crabs, and crayfish
ocean, lake, or pond beach, or aquarium with lobsters, shrimps,
    prawns, and crabs on display
adult helper

PROCEDURE

1. Look at the pictures in the book to see what lobsters,
   shrimps, prawns, crabs, and crayfish look like.
2. Take an adult to the beach or aquarium on a hunt for crabs
   or crayfish. If you are on an ocean beach, look in the sand and shallow
   water for pieces of crab shells to study. You might find a small crab under a
   rock in shallow water or in a **tide pool** (low area of ocean beach that traps
   water when the tide goes out). If you are on a lake or pond beach, look
   under rocks in shallow water for crayfish.
3. When you find a crab or a crayfish, pick it up by holding the sides of the
   shell between your thumb and finger. Watch how the animal uses its legs.
4. Study the shell. How is a crab shell different from a seashell?

EXPLANATION

Most shelled animals are **mollusks,** which means they have a soft body protected by a hard shell. These include oysters, clams, and snails. Lobsters,
shrimps, prawns, crabs, and crayfish are **crustaceans,** a group of animals that
have bodies covered with shells made of **segments** (sections). These segments
are held together by movable joints that allow the body to bend and the legs to
move. When crustaceans' bodies become too large for their shells, they shed
the shells and grow new ones. Prawns have thinner shells than crabs and lobsters. Lobsters and crabs have large front claws, or **pincers.**

Note: If you found a small crab, you can use it for the next experiment.

7

CRAB GUESS

How Is a Male Crab Distinguished from a Female?

MATERIALS

ocean beach

PROCEDURE

1. Search for small crabs under rocks on the beach.
2. When you find one, carefully pick it up by holding the sides of the shell between your thumb and finger.
3. Turn the crab over and examine the tail flap (see drawing).
4. Examine the tail flaps of several crabs. Do you notice any differences in the tail flaps?

EXPLANATION

Male crabs have a narrow, pointed tail flap with three segments. Female crabs have wider tail flaps with more than three segments.

SEAWEED CREATURES

What Lives in Seaweed?

MATERIALS

ocean beach at **low tide** (when the water is lowest on the beach)
face mask
seaweed
adult helper

PROCEDURE

1. Take an adult to the beach at low tide and look for a tide pool.
2. Use your face mask to look below the water for seaweed growing on a rock.
3. Carefully lift the seaweed. Do you see any tiny animals attached to the seaweed?

EXPLANATION

When you lifted the seaweed, you may have seen snails and crabs that have shed their shells and are hiding until their new shells harden. You may have discovered skeleton shrimps attached to the seaweed. Skeleton shrimps are about ½ to ¾ inches (1.3 to 2 cm) long with bodies that are **translucent** (able to allow some light to pass through). If you looked very closely, you may have discovered the tiny, dark eyes of opossum shrimps, which have bodies that are almost invisible against the seaweed.

SPINY SHELL

Why Does a Sea Urchin Have Spines?

MATERIALS

dead sea urchin (can be purchased in a shell
shop)

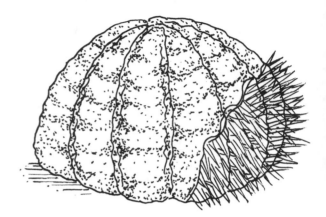

PROCEDURE

1. Feel the top of the sea urchin. What do you
   notice about the shell?
2. Examine the bottom of the sea urchin.
   What do you see?

EXPLANATION

The shell is round and has bumps. When the sea urchin was alive,
it had thousands of movable **spines** (sharp, stiff columns) growing from the bumps. The spines helped the sea urchin move
around in the ocean, bury itself in the sand, or burrow
under rocks. The spines also protected the sea urchin
from being eaten by fish. When you looked at the
underside of the sea urchin, you saw a mouth in the
center. The sea urchin used its five beaklike jaws to
nibble at seaweed and **barnacles** (small shellfish that
attach themselves to objects in seawater).

*Note: Never pick up a sea urchin on the beach, as it
could still be alive and its spines could hurt you.*

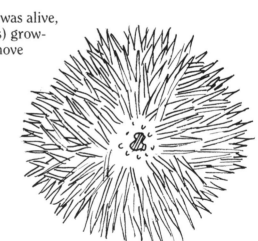

bottom

SAND CONE MAKERS

What Animals Make Small, Cone-Shaped Piles of Sand along the Edge of the Ocean?

MATERIALS

ocean beach

PROCEDURE

1. Walk along the beach by the waterline.
2. Look closely for tiny, cone-shaped piles of sand.
3. Examine the cones, then dig below the surface of the sand. What do you find?

EXPLANATION

Lugworms are sea worms that have many bristles on the sides of their body sections. Lugworms swallow sand and **digest** (break down) particles of food that are mixed with the sand. They push out the waste (mostly sand), which is formed into **casts,** the small, cone-shaped piles.

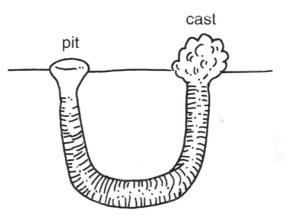

EGG FORMATION

Where Do Tadpoles Come From?

MATERIALS

pond
magnifying lens
pencil
notebook

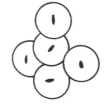

Note: Search for frog, toad,
    or newt eggs in the spring.

PROCEDURE

1. Search the pond weeds for leaves with small eggs deposited on them.
2. Examine the eggs closely using the magnifying lens.
3. Make detailed notes about the eggs, including the number found, the shape, and any other details you might find interesting to compare these eggs to other eggs. Be sure to draw a picture of the eggs.
4. Come back to the pond every few days to see if the eggs have hatched into tadpoles.

EXPLANATION

Frogs, toads, and newts are amphibians. **Amphibians** are animals that live underwater as babies, then breathe air as adults. After they hatch, tadpoles live in the water and have long tails and no legs. Soon, they grow legs, lose their long tails, and as adults move onto land.

MAYFLY NYMPHS

What Is a Mayfly?

MATERIALS

stream, river, or pond
shallow white dish
magnifying lens
new paintbrush

Note: This experiment is best done in spring.

PROCEDURE

1. Place about ¼ inch (0.6 cm) of stream, river, or pond water in the bottom of the dish.
2. Lift a stone lying near the water.
3. Examine the surface of the stone.
4. Gently brush the bottom of the stone over the dish of water.
5. Examine the water with the magnifying lens.

EXPLANATION

You probably found some mayfly **nymphs** (young) in the water. Mayflies are found in most streams and rivers throughout the world. They are also found in ponds and shallow lakes. Although their larvae live in water, the adults are delicate flying insects. Mayflies are useful in monitoring the quality of water, because their presence can be valuable indicators of the health of the water environment. They are also food for many fish.

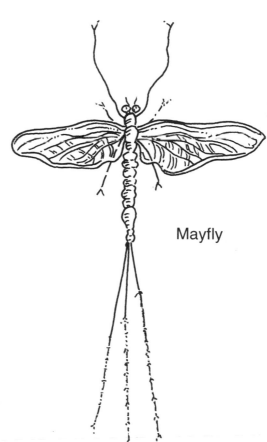

Mayfly

13

FISH

Fish are cold-blooded **vertebrates** (animals with backbones) with fins and gills. These creatures live in water.

In this section you will learn how fish skin is different from yours, and how fish breathe, swim, and hear.

SKIN AND SCALES

How Is a Fish's Skin Different from Yours?

MATERIALS

dead whole fish (from a fish market)
paper the fish was wrapped in
magnifying lens

Note: Get a kind of fish your family likes to eat.

PROCEDURE

1. Lay the fish on the paper it was wrapped in and examine its skin without the magnifying lens. Feel the fish's body.

2. Use the magnifying lens to examine the fish's skin. How is the fish's skin different from yours?

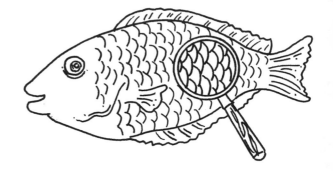

EXPLANATION

Most fish have an outer layer of curved **scales** (thin, flexible structures that overlap to form a protective covering). Fish scales are slimy. This helps fish slide more easily through the water. The scales also slide smoothly against each other, allowing fish to bend their bodies in any direction.

Note: You can use the same fish for the next two experiments. If you save the fish for the next day, wrap it in newspaper and store it in the refrigerator.

FISH EYES

Do Fish Close Their Eyes?

MATERIALS

dead whole fish (from a fish
      market) or a live fish in an
      aquarium
paper the market fish was
      wrapped in (if using market
      fish)

*Note: If you get a fish from the
      market, get a kind that your
      family likes to eat.*

PROCEDURE

1. If using a fish from the mar-
    ket, lay it on the paper it was
    wrapped in and look closely
    at its eyes. If the fish is in an aquarium, watch the fish's eyes for a minute
    or two.
2. Can you see eyelids on the market fish? Does the aquarium fish ever blink?

EXPLANATION

Fish never close their eyes, and they don't have eyelids. Their eyes are kept
clean and moist by the water around them.

Note: You can use the same dead fish for the next experiment.

DISSECTION INSPECTION

How Do Fish Breathe?

MATERIALS

dead whole fish (from a fish market) or
    a live fish in an aquarium
paper the market fish was wrapped in
    (if using market fish)

*Note: If you get a fish from the mar-
    ket, get a kind that your family likes to eat.*

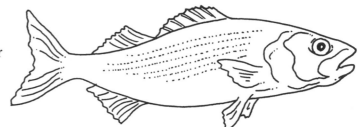

PROCEDURE

1. If using a fish from the market, lay it on the paper it was wrapped in and look closely at the two flaps located on each side of the fish behind the head. If the fish is in an aquarium, watch the two flaps on each side of the head move as the fish breathes.
2. Pull up on one of the flaps on the market fish and look underneath. Try to see inside the moving flaps of the aquarium fish. What do you see?

EXPLANATION

The flap is called the **operculum.** The areas underneath the flaps are **gills** (the fish's breathing organs). The gills of a live fish **expand** (open) and **contract** (flatten) as they remove **oxygen** (a colorless, odorless, tasteless gas) from the water and pass the oxygen into the fish's bloodstream. The gills of a live fish are red because they are filled with blood.

*Note: When you are done with this experiment, put the fish from the market
    in the refrigerator. Perhaps an adult would like to prepare it for dinner.*

WARM BLOOD, COLD BLOOD

Does a Fish Stay Warm in Cool Water?

MATERIALS

oral thermometer
ocean, lake, or pond
adult helper

PROCEDURE

1. Have an adult help you take your temperature. What is the reading on the thermometer?
2. Have the adult watch while you go into the water. Does the water seem cool at first?
3. Crouch in the water so you are in up to your neck.
4. Stay in the water for a few minutes, then get out and have the adult help you take your temperature again. What is the reading on the thermometer this time?

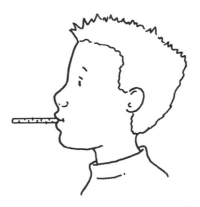

EXPLANATION

The water probably felt cool when you first went in, because its temperature was lower than your body temperature. Even though you spent time surrounded by cool water, your body temperature didn't change, or it changed only slightly. Humans are **warm-blooded,** meaning that your body works to keep your temperature the same no matter what the temperature is around you. Fish are **cold-blooded,** meaning that their bodies take on the temperature of the water surrounding them.

STRANGE FISH

Why Are Certain Ocean Fish Flat?

MATERIALS

aquarium exhibit that includes flounder (type of ocean fish)

PROCEDURE

1. Look closely at a flounder. What is the shape of its body?
2. Where are the flounder's eyes?

EXPLANATION

Flounder belong to a group of fish called **flatfish.** The bodies of these fish are very flat. A flounder also has both eyes on the same side of its head. When a flounder is hatched, it has an eye on

each side of its head, and its body is not flat. As the flounder grows, it moves to the bottom of the ocean floor and lies on one side. Its body gradually becomes flattened, and the eye on the bottom side gradually moves over the top of the head. Thus, the fish can still see the surrounding ocean with both eyes. The top side of the body takes on the color of the ocean water, and the underside of the body takes on the color of the ocean floor. Flounder sometimes cover their bodies with sand, leaving just their eyes uncovered.

DOLPHIN SOUNDS

How Do Dolphins Locate Food?

MATERIALS

yardstick (meterstick)
door

PROCEDURE

1. Stand 3 feet (1 m) away from the door.
2. Make a quick, sharp shout.
3. Open the door and make the same quick, sharp shout. How are the sounds different?

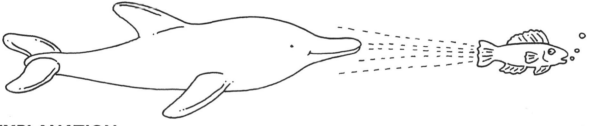

EXPLANATION

When you shouted with the door closed, your shout sounded louder than when you shouted with the door open. That's because with the door closed, the **sound waves** (vibrations of air caused by a moving object) from your voice were **reflected** (bounced back) right back to your ears. Dolphins make a variety of sounds like whistles, barks, and squeals. When they want to locate objects underwater, such as fish to eat, they use **echolocation** (reflection of sounds). In echolocation, the dolphin gives off a sound, then waits for the sound to bounce off an object and back to the dolphin's ears. This bounced sound is called an **echo.** The dolphin can tell by the time it takes the sound to come back how far away the object is. If you practiced, you could tell that you were near a closed door or wall even with your eyes closed, just by listening to the echo of your voice.

FLEXIBLE SWIMMING

How Do Fish Swim?

MATERIALS

dead whole fish (from a fish market)
paper the fish was wrapped in

PROCEDURE

1. Lay the fish on the paper it was wrapped in and pull away the outer portions of the fish to find the backbone. Observe how it is formed.
2. Hold the fish and move the backbone as much as possible. What do you notice?

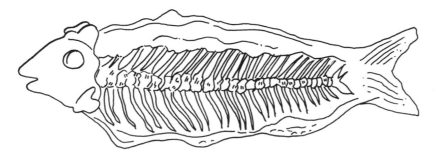

EXPLANATION

The backbone of the fish is formed from short sections of bone with cartilage (gristle) between each. This cartilage is flexible and can be moved from side to side. It will not, however, move easily up and down. When it was alive, the fish swam by shortening or contracting the muscles on each side of its backbone, making its whole body flex. The fish used this flexing motion and its fins to move through the water.

AQUARIUM NOTES

What Are a Fish's Patterns of Behavior?

MATERIALS

aquarium with fish, other water-
    dwelling animals, and plants
pen
notebook
library

PROCEDURE

1. Go to a public aquarium or
   arrange to spend some time
   watching an aquarium of a
   friend or in a pet store.

2. Every day spend several min-
   utes observing the fish. Watch how they move their mouths and what they
   do in order to move from one place to another. Observe their eyes.

3. Write down your observations in the notebook.

4. After observing for 5 days, study your notes. What have you learned about
   the habits of your fish? Continue to keep the notebook and research other
   habits of fish at the library.

EXPLANATION

By studying the fish, you soon discovered the patterns of behavior the fish had
established over a period of time. The study of animal behavior is called **ethology.**
It shows how animals interact with other animals. You may have observed that
fish and other animals sometimes use behaviors to threaten and scare off rivals
for their territories and their mates. Some fish must continually swim up to
breathe air on the surface of the water. Some may look like they are actually kiss-
ing one another. Some fish are more compatible with one another than others.

PIKE PREY

Do Fish Have a Form of Camouflage?

MATERIALS

slow-moving river
Polaroid sunglasses

Note: This experiment is best done on a sunny day.

PROCEDURE

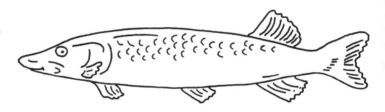

1. Before you put the sunglasses on, look for pike (a type of fish—see the drawing).
2. Now put the sunglasses on when you look for the fish. Can you find them any better?

EXPLANATION

It was not easy finding pike in the water without wearing sunglasses. Their green markings match the pattern of sunlight reflected on the water. These markings also blend in with the shadows in the weeds where they hide and wait for fish to eat. With the sunglasses on, you were able to see through the reflected sunlight. Thus, it was easier to see the fish under the water.

YOUNG RAYS

How Are Rays Hatched?

MATERIALS

ocean beach

Note: This experiment is best done in spring.

PROCEDURE

1. Search seaweeds and rock pools at low tide for egg cases of rays. The egg cases of these fish are rectangular, leathery sacs attached to seaweeds by tough threads. (See the drawing.)
2. When you find an egg case, hold it up to the light and see if you can find a young fish inside attached to the yolk sac.

EXPLANATION

If you were lucky, you could see the young fish inside attached to the yolk sac after you held the egg case to the light. This sac protects and nourishes the young ray until it is developed, which can take as long as 5 months.

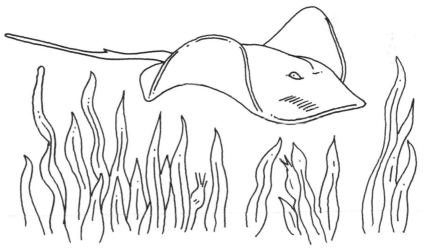

FUN AND GAMES

This section is filled with fun things to do in the water, so find an adult to keep watch, and put on your bathing suit! While you're having fun, you will be learning things like why your legs look stubby underwater, what happens when you talk underwater, and how whales spout.

SHORT, STUBBY LEGS

Why Do Your Legs Look Short and Stubby Underwater?

MATERIALS

clear lake or pond, or swimming pool
adult helper

PROCEDURE

1. Have the adult watch as you wade into the water until it is up to your waist. In a swimming pool, stand in the shallow end.
2. Look down through the water at your legs. What do you notice?

EXPLANATION

When you looked through the water at your legs, they looked short and stubby. When light rays enter the water, they bend, causing things under the water to look **distorted** (changed in shape).

28

WATER WALKING

Why Is It Hard to Walk in Water?

MATERIALS

ocean, lake, pond, or swimming pool
adult helper

PROCEDURE

1. Walk around on land. Observe the way you move through the air.
2. Have the adult watch as you go into the water until you are up to your hips.
3. Walk around in the water. How is this different from walking on land?
4. Try running in the water. What happens?

EXPLANATION

It is harder to walk through water than through air, because water is **denser.** This means water has more weight compared to its **volume** (the amount of space inside that has a length, width, and height) than air. The density of water makes the water resist the motion of your legs more than the air does. It is more difficult to run in water than to walk. Running requires bigger strides, which means you push against more water when you run in it.

TENNIS BALL SPRING

Why Does a Tennis Ball Fly into the Air When Released Underwater?

MATERIALS

tennis ball
ocean, lake, pond, or swimming pool
adult helper

PROCEDURE

1. Have an adult watch as you take the tennis ball into the water.
2. Push the tennis ball under the water and hold it there for a few seconds.
3. Let go of the ball. What happens?

EXPLANATION

The ball flew up into the air. Tennis balls are **buoyant** (able to float) because they contain air, which is lighter than water. They are held to the water's surface by **gravity** (the force that pulls everything toward the center of the earth). When you pushed the ball under the water, you **displaced** (pushed aside) the water. The upward force of buoyancy became greater than the downward force of gravity, so the ball flew up into the air when it was released.

FLOAT AND SINK

What Happens When Hollow Objects Are Pulled Underwater?

MATERIALS

ocean, lake, pond, swimming
    pool, or bathtub
hollow objects without lids,
    such as plastic cup, plas-
    tic bottle, empty soda can,
    plastic bowl
adult helper

PROCEDURE

1. Have the adult watch as you go into the water. If using a bathtub, you don't need to get into the tub. Just fill it half full with water.
2. Put the hollow objects on top of the water. What happens?
3. Push each object completely under the water and hold it there. What do you see?

EXPLANATION

When you put the hollow objects on top of the water, they looked empty and they floated. When you pushed the objects underwater, bubbles of air rose to the surface. The objects weren't really empty—they were full of air. Air is lighter than water, so it bubbled to the surface. Once the air left the objects, they filled up with water and sank.

AIR MATTRESS FLY

Why Does Your Air Mattress Fly Backward When You Jump Forward?

MATERIALS

air mattress
ocean, lake, pond, or swimming pool
adult helper

PROCEDURE

1. Have the adult watch as you take the air mattress into the water.
2. Crouch on top of the air mattress. Get ready to spring forward.
3. Spring forward off the air mattress into the water. What happens to the air mattress?

EXPLANATION

The air mattress shot backward as you jumped forward off it. There is a law of physics, called **Newton's third law of motion,** which says that for every action there is an equal but opposite reaction. When you pushed yourself forward, the air mattress was pushed backward with an equal amount of force.

SWIM FINS

How Do Swim Fins Work?

MATERIALS

ocean, lake, pond, or swimming pool
swim fins
adult helper

PROCEDURE

1. Have the adult watch while you swim around without the swim fins.
2. Put the swim fins on your feet and swim around again. What's different?

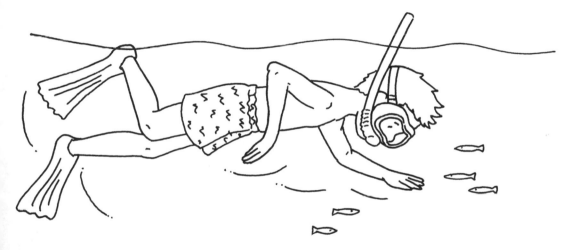

EXPLANATION

The swim fins helped you swim easier and faster. The swim fins have more **area** (surface space) than your feet. Because the swim fins can push more water when you kick, they give you more **propulsion** (forward push).

UNDERWATER TALK

What Happens When You Talk Underwater?

MATERIALS

ocean, lake, pond, or swimming
     pool
friend
adult helper

PROCEDURE

1. Have the adult watch as you
   and your friend go into the
   water.

2. Stand about 6 feet (2 m) away
   from your friend.

3. Together, you and your friend
   take a big breath and go underwater.

4. As you let out your breath
   under the water, say something to your friend. Listen while your friend
   says something to you. Can you and your friend understand each other?

EXPLANATION

Your voices were too garbled for you to understand each other. Sound waves
travel better through air than through water, because air has less density.
That's why scuba divers don't talk to one another underwater. They use hand
signals instead.

CHAMPION BREATH HOLDER

Can You Hold Your Breath Longer Than a Whale?

MATERIALS

ocean, lake, pond, or swimming pool
watch with a second hand, or a timer
adult helper

PROCEDURE

1. Have an adult watch as you go into the water up to your waist. In a swimming pool, stand in the shallow end.
2. Take a big breath, go underwater, and see how long you can stay under before you need to come up for air. Have your helper time you.
3. How long did you hold your breath?

EXPLANATION

You probably held your breath for less than a minute. Whales can hold their breath for over an hour! Whales are not fish, but **mammals,** as are people. Mammals are warm-blooded animals that have backbones. Female mammals give birth to live young and feed them with milk from mammary glands. Like people, whales can't breathe underwater. They must come to the surface to get air. A whale breathes through either one or two **blowholes** (slits that act as nostrils) located on the top of its head.

UNDERWATER UMBRELLA

How Is a Jellyfish Like an Umbrella?

MATERIALS

book with pictures of jellyfish, or jellyfish
    exhibit at an aquarium
old umbrella
lake, pond, or swimming pool
adult helper

PROCEDURE

1. Find out what jellyfish look like by looking at pictures in a book or visiting a jellyfish exhibit at an aquarium.
2. Have the adult watch as you take the *closed* umbrella into the water with you.
3. Stand with the umbrella straight up.
4. Take a big breath and go underwater, taking the umbrella with you.
5. Come back up and open the umbrella, holding it just above your head.
6. Take another big breath and go under, trying to pull the umbrella under with you. What happens?

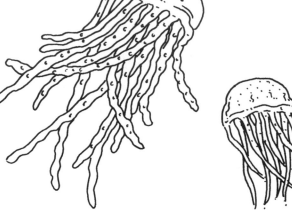

EXPLANATION

Some jellyfish are shaped like an umbrella. Their shape when they're "open" helps slow down their rate of sinking. They can change their shape, like closing an umbrella, by contracting their muscles. As they close up, like an umbrella, the water inside the "umbrella" is squeezed downward, which pushes the jellyfish up faster.

Note: If you see a jellyfish on the beach, don't touch it. If it is alive, it could sting you.

PLANTS

Plants are many-celled living things that usually make their own food. (A **cell** is the basic unit of all plants and animals.) Plants are the most important food source for life on Earth. Plant life is abundant throughout the world, but only certain kinds of plants live in or near the water.

How do plants make oxygen? What is bladder wrack? How does seaweed stick to rocks? Find out in this section.

PLANT OXYGEN

How Is Oxygen Made in Oceans, Lakes, and Ponds?

MATERIALS

romaine lettuce leaf
jar
water
bowl
cardboard larger than mouth of jar

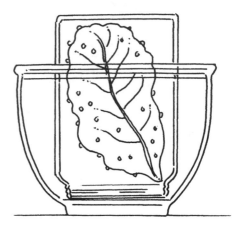

PROCEDURE

1. Put the romaine lettuce leaf in the jar and fill the jar with water to the very top.
2. Fill the bowl at least half full with water.
3. Place a piece of cardboard over the mouth of the jar.
4. Holding the cardboard in place, quickly turn the jar upside down into the bowl of water. Once the jar mouth is underwater, take the cardboard away. The jar should stay full of water as it sits upside down in the bowl.
5. Place the bowl in a sunny spot and let it sit.
6. Check the lettuce in 2 hours. Look at the leaf very closely. What do you see?

EXPLANATION

There were bubbles on the lettuce leaf. The bubbles were filled with oxygen. Plants take in **carbon dioxide** (a gas breathed out by people and animals) and make oxygen. **Algae** (plants in oceans, lakes, and ponds) make oxygen that fish and other **aquatic** (water) animals need. Plants are just one source of aquatic oxygen. Oxygen is also added to the water by the action of waves, wind, and rain.

WATER COLOR

How Does Algae Affect the Color of Water in Oceans, Lakes, and Ponds?

MATERIALS

sheet of colored plastic wrap
small clear or white bowl
water

PROCEDURE

1. Place the sheet of colored plastic wrap in the bowl and open out the edges of the wrap so they lie over the rim of the bowl.
2. Pour water on top of the plastic wrap, so the wrap is between the water and the bottom of the bowl.
3. Look down at the water. What color does the water seem to be?

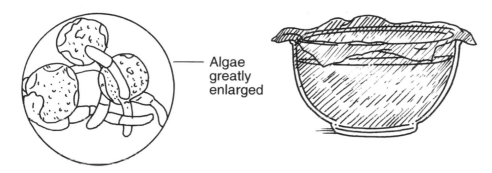

Algae greatly enlarged

EXPLANATION

The water looked the same color as the plastic. A large amount of algae in water makes the water look like it is the color of the algae. Algae in lakes and ponds can make the water look green. Algae in the ocean is called seaweed. It can sometimes make whole areas of water appear to be red, brown, or green.

LIVING COLOR

How Many Different Colors and Kinds of Seaweed Can You Find?

MATERIALS

snorkeling gear (optional)
ocean beach
adult helper

PROCEDURE

1. Get an adult to take you snorkeling in the ocean or for a walk on the beach.
2. Look for seaweed. (On the beach, look in areas of shallow water where there are rocks, or in tide pools.)
3. How many different colors and kinds of seaweed can you find?

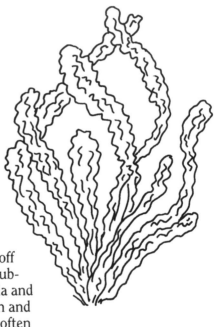

EXPLANATION

Brown seaweed is found in cold waters, like those off the coast of Massachusetts. Red algae is found in subtropical waters, like those off the coast of California and in the New York harbor. **Sea lettuce** is bright green and looks a lot like the lettuce in salads. Sea lettuce is often found attached to rocks in **estuaries** (ocean inlets). You might also find sea lettuce floating in the ocean or washed up on the beach. **Bladder wrack,** also called **rockweed,** has forked, brownish-green **fronds** (leaves). Bladder wrack grows over rocks in the ocean or in tide pools.

Note: If you found bladder wrack, you may want to do the next experiment, too.

BLADDER WRACK POP

What Are the Distinguishing Characteristics of Bladder Wrack?

MATERIALS

ocean beach at low tide
face mask
adult helper

PROCEDURE

1. Take an adult to the beach at low tide and look for a tide pool.
2. Use your face mask to look below the water for bladder wrack growing on a rock (see the drawing).

Note: If you found bladder wrack during the last experiment, look in the area where you found it.

3. Look closely at the fronds of the bladder wrack for small bumps.
4. Squeeze one of the bumps between your fingers. What happens?

EXPLANATION

The bumps are air-filled **bladders** (sacs) that popped when you squeezed them. The bladders are where the plant cells are making new plants, which will be released into the water to grow on their own.

STICKY SEAWEED

How Does Seaweed Stick to Rocks?

MATERIALS

ocean beach at low tide
adult helper

PROCEDURE

1. Take an adult to the beach at low tide and look on the beach, in the water, or in a tide pool for seaweed growing on a rock or shell.

2. Try to pull the seaweed off the rock or shell. What happens?

EXPLANATION

You were unable to pull the seaweed off the rock or shell. Seaweed will break before it can be pulled free of the rock. The rootlike structures that hold the seaweed to the rock aren't true roots, but **holdfasts.** The holdfasts have cells that make a sticky substance, sort of like glue, that bonds the holdfasts to rocks or shells.

SEAWEED FORECAST

How Can Seaweed Forecast the Weather?

MATERIALS

ocean beach
string
adult helper

PROCEDURE

1. Have an adult help you find and gather a few long pieces of seaweed from the beach or ocean.
2. Tie a string around the bottom of the seaweed and hang the seaweed, upside down, outside.
3. Check the seaweed several hours later by touching it. Does it feel damp or dry?

EXPLANATION

When the air is very moist, the seaweed will **absorb** (soak up) some of the moisture and feel damp. This means that it is likely to rain. If the air is dry, the air will absorb moisture from the seaweed, drying it out. This means that it's not going to rain soon.

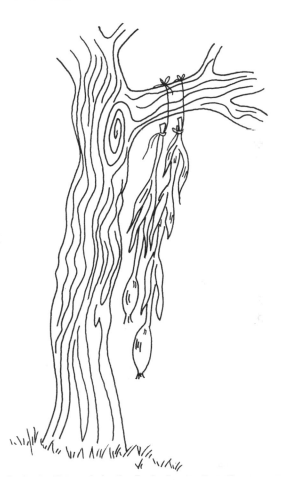

PLANT FOOD

Is Seaweed Edible?

MATERIALS

grocery store or your kitchen

PROCEDURE

1. Go to the grocery store or look inside the refrigerator and cabinets of your kitchen.

2. Read the ingredients labels on ice creams, jellies, soups, and sauces, looking for the word *agar*. Have you eaten any foods that have agar as an ingredient?

EXPLANATION

Agar is a substance prepared from the cell wall of **red algae** (a seaweed that makes its own food).
The algae is washed and dried, and the agar is **extracted** (taken from) the algae with boiling water. As it cools, the agar forms a **gel** (jelly). This gel is used to thicken ice creams, jellies, gelatins, soups, and sauces. You've probably been eating seaweed without knowing it!

SEASONAL PICTURE

How Do Environments Surrounding Water Change during the Seasons?

MATERIALS

pond, stream, or riverbank
camera

PROCEDURE

1. Find a place where a great deal of plant life surrounds the water.
2. Take a picture of the **vegetation** (plants) in the spring.
3. Find the same area and take a picture during the summer and then during the autumn and winter.
4. After all four pictures have been taken, compare them.

EXPLANATION

The vegetation was different in each picture. The spring gives plants more sunlight each day and temperatures rise. This is the beginning of life for many new plants and animals. **Dormant** (resting) plants soak up the sun's light, **transforming** (changing) it into food. Water plants provide food for the many animals living in the water, as well as places to live, hide, and lay eggs. Plants blossom throughout the summer, showing a variety of colors. As summer gradually ends, daylight shortens and the nights become cooler. This causes life in the water to slow down and prepare for winter. Animals find their places of shelter and **hibernate** (rest) under the water and in plant **debris** (waste). Plants become brown and finally shed much of their **foliage** (leaves), becoming dormant once again.

WATER LILY FLOAT

How Does a Water Lily Remain Floating?

MATERIALS

3-inch (7.5-cm) square of waxed paper
3-inch (7.5-cm) square of tissue paper
bowl of water
eyedropper
water lily

PROCEDURE

1. Examine the surface of the papers.
2. Place the waxed paper and the tissue paper on the surface of the water.
3. Suction some water into the eyedropper.
4. Drop a droplet of water on each piece of paper. What happens?
5. Study the leaves of a water lily. What do you notice about the surface covering of the leaves?

EXPLANATION

After a short period of time, the tissue paper sank but the waxed paper kept floating. The waxed paper is coated with a waxy substance that **repels** (pushes away) water. A water lily leaf is also coated with a waxy substance. Each leaf also has a slit in it that allows water to drain from the surface. This keeps water from building up on top and pushing the flower down.

POND PLANTS

What Types of Plants Grow in Ponds?

MATERIALS

pond
magnifying lens
field guide to weeds and grasses
adult helper

PROCEDURE

1. Bring an adult to a pond and select a spot on the bank for investigating.

2. With the magnifying lens, observe the different types of plant life that live alongside the pond. Notice how the plants on dry land are different from those in the water. Observe the plants that bloom, are in bud, and have different characteristics. Look at their leaves and try to see if any animal life is living among them.

3. Look up the types of plants you find in the field guide.

EXPLANATION

You probably saw several wetland plants. (**Wetland** is land soaked with water.) The most familiar are cattails, with their swaying brown flower clusters. They are found at the edges of ponds, rivers, lakes, or nearly anyplace where there is shallow, standing water. They can grow up to 5 feet (1½ m) high. The most interesting part of cattails is their flowers. Each cattail has thousands of tiny brown flowers all tightly **compressed** (squeezed together) on the top of its stems. In late summer and early fall, these flowers come apart, releasing their seeds into the wind. You may also have found some sedges. **Sedges** are **perennial** (growing back each year) herbs found in most freshwater wetlands. They look like grasses, but are very different. The easiest way to tell a sedge from a grass is by feeling the stem. The stem on grass is flat or rounded. The stem on a sedge is triangular.

SALT WATER

The largest bodies of water on our Earth, the oceans, contain salt.

In this section you will learn interesting facts about the oceans, including where the salt came from, how to get salt out of ocean water, why oceans don't freeze, and what causes tides.

OCEAN TASTE

How Does Ocean Water Taste?

MATERIALS

ocean beach
adult helper

PROCEDURE

1. Have the adult watch as you wade into the ocean.
2. Dip your finger in the water.
3. Lick your finger. How does the water taste?

EXPLANATION

The water tasted salty. Salt is made up of two **elements** (substances that can't be broken down by chemical action). These elements, sodium and chlorine, are found in some rocks and soils. Rain washes over these rocks and soils, picks up a little sodium and chlorine, and carries them into the rivers. This process causes the sodium and chlorine to mix and form **sodium chloride,** which is the chemical name for salt. Rivers have been carrying salt into the oceans for millions of years.

SALT SOURCE

How Can Salt Be Removed from Ocean Water?

MATERIALS

ocean water or about 10 tablespoons (150 ml) salt dis-
    solved in 1 cup (250 ml) water
aluminum pie pan
clock, watch, or timer
magnifying lens

Note: This experiment is best done on a sunny day.

PROCEDURE

1. Pour a thin layer of the ocean water or salt water
    into the aluminum pie pan, just enough to cover
    the bottom.
2. Place the pan in the sun.
3. Check the pan after an hour and add more salt water, if needed, to keep the
    bottom covered.
4. Check the pan several hours later to see if the water is gone. When all the
    water is gone, look closely at the bottom of the pan. What do you see?
5. Wet your finger, then touch the white matter in the bottom of the pan.
    Lick your finger. What does it taste like?
6. Look at the white matter with the magnifying lens. What do you see?

EXPLANATION

The water **evaporated** (changed to a gas) into the air, leaving a white **residue**
(remaining matter) on the bottom of the pan. When you tasted it, you knew it
was the salt that had been in the water. Ocean water is one source of salt.
When you looked through the magnifying lens, you noticed the salt was
formed into square **crystals** (regularly shaped pieces formed by many substances when they become solids). Salt crystals are always square.

51

OCEAN FREEZE

Does Ocean Water Freeze As Quickly As Drinking Water?

MATERIALS

2 paper or Styro-
    foam cups
ocean water
tap water
marking pen
freezer
adult helper

PROCEDURE

1. Fill one of the cups half full with ocean water and use the marker to label it "salt water."

Note: If you go into the ocean to get the water, ask an adult to watch.

2. Fill the other cup half full with tap water and use the marker to label it "tap water."

3. Place the cups in the freezer and check them again in an hour. What do you notice?

EXPLANATION

The cup of tap water was more frozen than the cup of salt water. Water with salt in it freezes at a lower temperature than water without salt. The salt in the ocean keeps most of the ocean from freezing in winter. The surface of the ocean freezes around the North and South Poles, where it is extremely cold, but water deep under the surface doesn't freeze.

TIDE INS AND OUTS

What Is a Tide?

MATERIALS

sandy ocean beach

PROCEDURE

1. Walk along the beach, looking at the sand above the waterline.
2. Is it wet or dry? Can you think why?

EXPLANATION

All oceans have tides. **Tides** are changes in the water level caused by changes in the **gravitational attraction** (pull of gravity) of the earth and moon. If the tide is coming in, the water is slowly covering more of the dry beach. If the tide is going out, the water is dropping away from the beach, leaving the sand wet above the waterline.

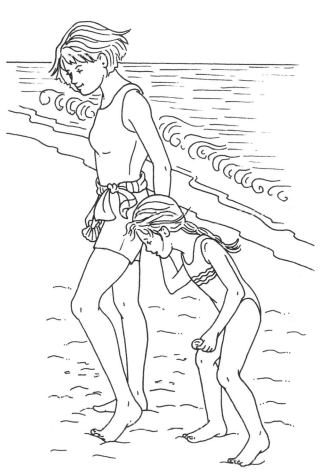

OCEAN ISLES

Do Islands Form Underwater?

MATERIALS

wet sand
sand shovel

PROCEDURE

1. Shape some wet sand into the shape of a cone.
   Observe the top of the cone.
2. Use the shovel to slice off the top of the cone.
   How does the top of the cone look now?

EXPLANATION

At first the cone was the same shape as a
seamount (a volcano that has risen from the
ocean floor but has not reached the surface).
When you sliced off the top, the cone was the
shape of a **guyot** (a seamount that has risen to
the surface of the ocean and formed an island).
Over millions of years, the base of a guyot can
sink slowly into the ocean floor, and the
island will become a flat-topped,
underwater mountain.

CORAL REEF BARRIERS

How Do Coral Reefs Protect the Beach?

MATERIALS

ruler
water
rectangular cake pan
play sand
gravel
piece of cardboard about 1 inch
    (2.5 cm) narrower than the
    cake pan

PROCEDURE

1. Pour 2 inches (5 cm) of water into the pan.
2. Mound sand near one end of the pan to make an island.
3. Completely surround the island with a wall of gravel.
4. At the other end of the pan, use the cardboard to make waves in the water. What happens to the sand?
5. Take the gravel out of the cake pan.
6. Make more waves. What happens to the sand now?

EXPLANATION

When the gravel was in place, it kept the sand from being washed away by the waves. When you took the gravel away, the waves washed sand away from the mound. Coral reefs that lie offshore, parallel to the coastline, are called **barrier reefs.** These barrier reefs protect the beaches in much the same way that the gravel protected the sand in the experiment.

WATER FLOAT

Is It Easier to Float in the Ocean or a Swimming Pool?

MATERIALS

drinking glass
tap water
fresh egg
table salt
tablespoon

PROCEDURE

1. Fill the glass half full with tap water.
2. Slowly and carefully place the egg in the water. What happens?
3. Add the salt to the water 1 tablespoon (15 ml) at a time. Continue adding salt until the egg floats.
4. When the egg floats, slowly fill the glass almost full with water by dribbling spoonfuls of tap water down the side of the glass. This must be done slowly so the waters do not mix. What happens to the egg when the glass is almost full?

EXPLANATION

When you put the egg in the glass of tap water, it sank to the bottom because an egg is denser than freshwater. When you added salt to the water, the egg floated because an egg is less dense than salt water. When you slowly added more tap water to the glass, the egg appeared to float in the middle of the glass. It was actually floating on the salt water, which had a layer of tap water above it. In the same way, it is easier for a person to float in the ocean's salt water than in the water in a swimming pool.

SAND AND ROCKS

Sand is loose, gritty grains of rock. The color of sand depends on the kind of rock the grains came from. Sand covers many of the world's beaches.

In this section you will find out why sand sticks together when wet, how sand can clean water, and where sand dunes come from.

SAND BEGINNINGS

How Is Sand Made?

MATERIALS

paper towel
2 rocks with rough edges

PROCEDURE

1. Lay the paper towel on a flat surface.
2. Scrape the rocks together over the paper towel. What do you see on the paper towel?

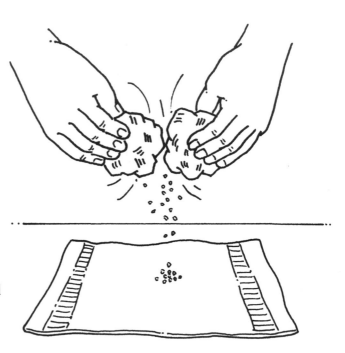

EXPLANATION

Scraping the rocks together made grains of sand on the paper towel. Sand is made by **erosion** (the wearing away of rocks by running water, rain, waves, and wind). It took millions of years to make all the sand on the beaches.

COLOR EXAM

What Color Is Sand?

MATERIALS

sandy ocean beach
sand sifter (helpful, not required)
piece of white cardboard for dark sand, or piece
    of dark cardboard for light sand
magnifying lens
tweezers

PROCEDURE

1. Shake a small amount of sand through a sand sifter onto the cardboard. If
you don't have a sifter, remove litter, stones, and pieces of seaweed from
the sand by hand.

2. Look at the sand through the magnifying lens.

3. Use the tweezers to separate the sand
grains. What colors are the grains?

EXPLANATION

Sand is made of **minerals,** which are elements or **compounds**
(combinations of two substances) with a crystal-like structure. Most minerals
in sand are **quartz,** which is also found in **granite** (hard, igneous rocks). Quartz
can be colorless, white, rose, brown, violet, smoky, or other colors. If you saw
any red grains, they were most likely the common mineral **garnet.** Thin, black,
flaky grains were probably **mica.** Another common mineral, **hornblende,** is a
black, rectangular crystal. Any green crystals you saw were probably **olivine,** a
mineral common in **meteorites** (rocks from space that landed on Earth). Some
beaches have mostly brown sand and others have mostly white sand, depending on the kinds of rocks the sand came from. In tropical areas, crushed
seashells make the sand look pink. Beaches where the sand was formed from
volcanoes can even look green or black.

BLACK GRAINS

What Happens When a Magnet Is Passed through Sand?

MATERIALS

magnet
sandy beach

PROCEDURE

1. Run the magnet through the sand.
2. What do you see on the magnet when you remove it from the sand?

EXPLANATION

The magnet may have picked up grains of **micrometeorites,** tiny, black, dustlike matter from space. Billions of micrometeorites have fallen to Earth. Micrometeorite particles are attracted to magnets.

MAGNIFIED GRAINS

What Is between Grains of Dry Sand?

MATERIALS

pebbles
plastic bowl
water

PROCEDURE

1. Put the pebbles in the bowl. Observe the spaces between the pebbles.
2. Cover the pebbles with water. What happens to the spaces between the pebbles?

EXPLANATION

The pebbles in the bowl are like big grains of sand. The pebbles have air spaces between them, just as dry grains of sand do. When you covered the pebbles with water, the water filled in the air spaces. This is what happens when you wet sand.

WET SAND, DRY SAND

Why Does Sand Stick Together When It Is Wet?

MATERIALS

wet sand
2 small margarine tubs or other
    plastic containers
dry sand

PROCEDURE

1. Pack wet sand into one container until it is full.
2. Pack dry sand in another container until it is full.
3. Turn each container over and remove the container. What happens?

EXPLANATION

The wet sand stuck together and held the shape of the container, while the dry sand did not. Sand sticks together when it is wet because of two forces. One is the water's **cohesion,** meaning that like **molecules** (the smallest parts of elements) are attracted to each other. The other force is **adhesion,** the attraction between two substances. The water molecules cohere to each other, and the water adheres to the sand. This keeps the wet sand together.

EASY CLEAN

Can Sand Clean Water?

MATERIALS

piece of cheesecloth (available at a hardware store)
1-foot (30-cm) length of PVC pipe (available at a hardware store)
duct tape (available at a hardware store)
ruler   mud
play sand   water
small and large gravel   2 plastic buckets

PROCEDURE

1. Hold a double layer of cheesecloth over one end of the pipe. Tape the cloth securely to the pipe by wrapping tape over the edges of the cheesecloth and around the pipe.

2. Pour 2 inches (5 cm) of sand into the open end of the pipe (the sand will lie against the cheesecloth).

3. Put 2 inches (5 cm) of small gravel on top of the sand, and 2 inches (5 cm) of large gravel on top of the small gravel.

4. Mix mud and water in one bucket.

5. Hold the pipe over the empty bucket, with the cheesecloth-covered end of the pipe down.

6. Pour the muddy water into the top of the pipe and catch the water in the second bucket. What do you notice about the water in the second bucket?

EXPLANATION

The muddy water was made cleaner by its trip through the gravel and sand. The gravel and sand **filtered** (cleaned) the water by catching the particles of mud in the water, which are larger and heavier than water molecules.

63

SAND WATCH

What Is a Sandbar?

MATERIALS

sandy beach at the ocean or at a large lake

PROCEDURE

1. Stand on the beach and watch the waves roll in.
2. Count the number of times the waves break (come in and stop) before they reach the shoreline. Do they break once or twice?

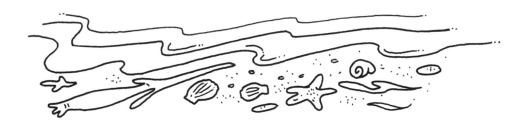

EXPLANATION

Waves always break once, near the shoreline. If you see an area where the waves break an extra time, that means there is a **sandbar** (long ridge of sand and gravel) under the water. Sandbars lie parallel to the shore and are usually seen only at low tide. But if you watch the waves carefully for the extra break, you can tell where the sandbars are.

Note: Don't wade out to a sandbar unless it is close to shore and you take an adult with you.

WARM SAND, COOL SAND

Why Is Sand Warm on Top of the Beach, but Cool Underneath?

MATERIALS

sand shovel
sandy beach

PROCEDURE

1. Dig a hole about 1 foot (30 cm) deep in the sand.
2. Feel the sand at the bottom of the hole.
3. Feel the top layer of sand on the beach. How does the top layer feel compared to the sand at the bottom of the hole?

EXPLANATION

In the summer, the top layer of sand on the beach felt warmer than the sand at the bottom of the hole.

The sand on the surface is warmed by the sun, but the sand at the bottom of the hole is cool because it is **insulated** (protected from the passage of heat) by the sand above it. The temperature of the top layer of sand changes with the air temperature, but the temperature of any sand deeper than 1½ feet (45 cm) stays the same year-round.

65

SMOOTH ROCKS

How Do Beach and River Rocks Become Smooth?

MATERIALS

piece of hard candy in a wrapper (or enclosed in plastic wrap)
hammer
cold tap water

PROCEDURE

1. Tap the wrapped candy with the hammer to break the candy, leaving at least one large piece with a sharp edge.
2. Unwrap one of the sharp-edged pieces.
3. Feel the sharp edge, then hold it under cold running water. What happens to the edge as the water runs over it?

EXPLANATION

The water smoothed out the sharp edge of the candy. The constant battering of waves against rocky cliffs causes some rocks to break off and fall to the beach, where they are constantly washed over by the waves.
This movement of water wears off the sharp edges of the rocks, making them smooth and somewhat rounded. Water in rivers rolls rocks along the bottom, giving them a rounded shape.

ROCK COLLECTION

What Kinds of Rocks Are Found on the Beach?

MATERIALS

ocean, lake, pond, or river beach
beach pail
rock reference book
adult helper

PROCEDURE

1. Take an adult for a walk on the beach.
2. Look on the beach and in shallow water for rocks.
3. Use the pail to collect several rocks that look different from one other.
4. Try to identify your rocks by comparing them to the ones in the reference book.

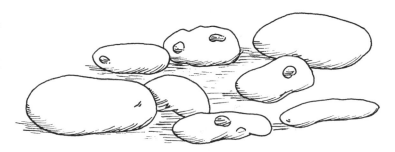

EXPLANATION

The scientific way to group your rocks is by type (they may do this in the reference book). It's also interesting to group them by shape. Granite is an **igneous rock,** a very hard rock that produces ball-shaped pebbles. Igneous rocks are formed by great heat under the earth's surface. **Sedimentary rocks** are formed by matter pressing together, and **metamorphic rocks** are formed by heat or pressure. Both sedimentary and metamorphic rocks split into slabs, producing disks. **Quartzite** (a rock formed by crystallizing sandstone) sometimes produces cigar-shaped pebbles after being constantly rolled around by the water.

67

DELTA FORMATION

How Are Deltas Formed?

MATERIALS

about 10 tablespoons (150 ml) coarse sand
deep clear plastic bowl
water
wooden spoon

PROCEDURE

1. Put all of the sand in the bowl.
2. Slowly pour the water into the bowl until it is half full.
3. Without touching the spoon to the sand, quickly stir the water. What do you notice about the sand?
4. Remove the spoon and watch the sand. What do you notice about the sand particles?

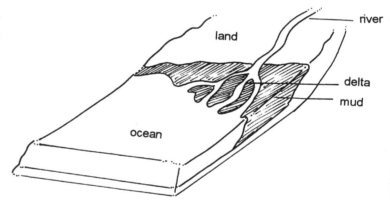

EXPLANATION

When you stirred the water, the swirling water picked up particles of sand. When the water slowed down, the particles began to settle. Moving water carries particles of sand and other debris. River water takes a variety of materials with it. At the mouth of the river, the water slows down and the materials settle. **Sediments** (matter that settles) are carried downstream and can build up at the mouths of rivers. These areas formed by deposits are called **deltas.**

SHELLS

Shells are the hard, outer coverings of certain animals, called mollusks. Mollusks grow shells to protect themselves from **predators** (animals that kill for food). You can find a wide variety of shells on an ocean beach, but there are lake and pond animals that grow shells, too.

This section explores the different kinds of mollusks that grow shells. Have you ever heard of a right-handed snail?

SNAILS, SNAILS, SNAILS

How Do Snail Shells Grow?

MATERIALS

ocean, lake, or pond beach
plastic bucket
adult helper

PROCEDURE

1. Take an adult with you to the beach.
2. Look in shallow water or tide pools at the ocean, or at the edges of the water at the lake or pond, for empty, spiral-shaped shells shaped like the ones in the drawing.
3. Collect the empty shells in the bucket.
4. Examine the parts of the shells. How many different parts can you see?

EXPLANATION

The shells are snail shells. There are many different kinds of snails, or **gastropods.** Gastropods belong to a division of animals called mollusks, soft-bodied animals that grow a shell to protect themselves. Gastropods grow hard, spiral-shaped shells. Most gastropod shells have a pointy end, called the **spire.** A few ocean snail shells don't have spires. The rounded hump in the shell is the place that the snail last lived. The opening of the shell is where the snail sticks out its head and single foot so it can travel to find food.

Note: Use the shells for the next experiment.

RIGHT AND LEFT SNAILS

Do All Snail Shells Coil in the Same Direction?

MATERIALS

collection of snail shells (from previous experiment)
2 large plastic cups

PROCEDURE

1. Pick up a shell and hold it so that its spire is pointing up and the opening is facing you.

2. Look closely inside the opening to see which direction the shell curves inside. If your right hand were small enough to fit inside the shell, would your fingers be able to curl around the inside of the curve? If the answer is yes, you are holding a right-handed snail shell. If the answer is no, you are holding a left-handed snail shell.

3. Examine all the shells in the same manner. Put all the right-handed shells in one cup and all the left-handed shells in the other cup. Which cup has the most shells?

EXPLANATION

If all your snail shells were the same kind, they would all end up in the same cup. All snail shells grow in a spiral shape and are either right-handed or left-handed, depending on the kind of snail that grew the shell. Pond snails grow right-handed shells. Shells of ocean **conchs** (shellfish with a large spiral-shaped shell) are right-handed, but shells of some ocean **whelks** (small snails with spiral shells) are left-handed.

71

THE DISAPPEARING SHELL

What Are Seashells?

MATERIALS

tiny empty shell
jar
vinegar

*Note: If you go into the water to look for a
shell, ask an adult to watch you.*

PROCEDURE

1. Put the empty shell in the jar.
2. Pour in vinegar to a depth that covers the shell. What happens in the jar?
3. Leave the jar to sit, and check it again a few hours later. What happened to the shell?

EXPLANATION

When you first poured in the vinegar, gas bubbles formed. Then, hours later, the shell disappeared. Animals that live in the sea absorb **calcium carbonate,** a white crystal-like compound found in seawater. The animals use this calcium carbonate to build their shells. Vinegar contains an **acid** (substance that can eat away metals and sometimes burn skin). When the acid in the vinegar came in contact with the shell, the acid began **dissolving** (mixing completely with a liquid) the calcium carbonate, releasing gas bubbles. After a few hours, the acid in the vinegar dissolved all of the calcium carbonate.

SUN SHY

Why Do Snails Hide from the Sun?

MATERIALS

ocean, lake, or pond beach
plastic cup
magnifying lens
adult helper

PROCEDURE

1. Take an adult with you to the beach.
2. Look in shallow water or tide pools at the ocean, or at the edges of the water at the lake or pond, for live snails.
3. Collect 1 or 2 snails in the cup, being sure to pick up and handle the snails carefully.
4. Lay the snails in a sunny spot on the beach. What do they do?
5. Wait 2 minutes and examine the opening of the shell with the magnifying lens. What do you see?

Note: When you've finished the experiment, carefully put the snails back where you found them.

EXPLANATION

Snails need to stay moist, so the snails you placed in the sun hid inside their shells to keep from drying out. Sometimes snails will plug up the openings of their shells, sealing themselves inside.

ALGAE TRAILS

What Kind of Animal Leaves Trails in Algae?

MATERIALS

ocean beach
adult helper

PROCEDURE

1. Take a walk with an adult on the beach, looking for algae-covered rocks.
2. Look for little lines, or trails, in the algae.
3. If you find trails, look for tent-shaped shells nearby.

EXPLANATION

The trails were made by **limpets,** gastropods that have tent-shaped shells. They move across the algae, eating it and leaving little trails behind. Like other gastropods, limpets have one large, thick suction foot that clings to objects such as rocks. Limpets can also be found on small seaweed.

SHELL DWELLER

What Animal Lives in Abandoned Empty Shells?

MATERIALS

ocean beach
magnifying lens
adult helper

PROCEDURE

1. At low tide, have an adult watch as you wade into water just over your ankles.
2. Look for snail shells like the ones in the drawing.
3. Pick up the shells very carefully. Look in the opening, using the magnifying lens.
4. When you find a shell that has an animal in it that isn't a snail, carefully lay the shell on the sand just above the waterline and watch what happens.

Note: Be careful not to harm the creature inside the shell.

EXPLANATION

When you put the shell down on the sand, the creature inside probably moved back to the water. It either left the shell or carried it on its back. A creature in a shell that isn't a snail is probably a **hermit crab.** These crabs are called hermits because they live alone. Hermit crabs do not make their own shells, but live in shells left behind by other animals, especially snails.

Note: If your crab stayed in the shell, or if you picked up a real snail, carefully put it back where you found it.

75

SHELL GAME

What Happens When a Hermit Crab Finds a Larger Shell?

MATERIALS

ocean beach at low tide
bucket
small empty aquarium or large glass baking
    dish with straight sides
ruler
adult helper

PROCEDURE

1. Have the adult watch as you wade into the
ocean and collect some seawater in the bucket.
2. Pour seawater into the aquarium or dish to a depth of about 1 inch (2.5 cm).
3. Have the adult watch as you wade into the ocean and add about 1 inch (2.5 cm) of water to the bucket.
4. Collect some hermit crabs in shells (see previous experiment for how to do this) and put them in the bucket.
5. Collect some empty shells a little bigger than the shells your crabs already have.
6. Put the crabs in the aquarium. Add the empty shells. What happens?

EXPLANATION

The hermit crabs may have moved to the empty shells or exchanged shells with other crabs. As hermit crabs grow, they must find bigger shells. A hermit crab changes shells many times in its life.

Note: When you're finished with this experiment, take the crabs to a shallow place in the water and release them.

SEA SOUNDS

Why Do You Seem to Hear the Ocean in Empty Shells?

MATERIALS

large, empty conch (gastropod) shell (can't always be found on the ocean
    beach, but is available in a shell shop—see illustration)

Note: If you go into the water to look for shells, ask an adult to watch you.

PROCEDURE

1. Hold the open end of the conch shell to your ear.
2. Listen closely. What do you hear?

EXPLANATION

You heard something that sounded like the
roaring of the ocean. Seashells do not make
any sounds of their own. Inside the conch
shell are lots of curves which reflect sound.
These reflections are called echoes. What
you heard were the sounds of many echoes.

OYSTERS AND CLAMS

What Lives in Shells with Two Halves?

MATERIALS

ocean or lake beach
adult helper

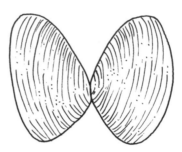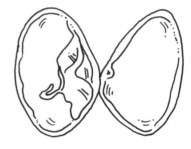

PROCEDURE

1. Search the beach, or have an adult watch as you wade in the water, looking for an empty shell with two halves.
2. Shut the shell, or if the "hinge" that holds the two halves together is broken, fit the two halves together.
3. What does the shape of the shell tell you about the animal that lived there?
4. Look for rings on the outside of the shell. What might they tell you about the animal's age?

EXPLANATION

Oysters and clams are bivalves, meaning that their shells are made of two halves. The two valves are connected by a hinge. The shell must open for the animal to eat and breathe. The animal in the shell can protect itself by holding the valves closed, using two strong muscles. When a bivalve is **spawned** (emerges from the egg), it may be only 1/12 inch (0.2 cm) long. The bivalve begins growing a shell immediately. The rings on the shell you found show the growth pattern of the animal. By looking at the rings, you can see how big the shell was at all the different stages of the bivalve's life.

Note: Use the bivalve shell for the next experiment.

BIVALVE LOOK

What Does the Inside of a Bivalve Reveal?

MATERIALS

empty bivalve shell
    (from previous experiment)

PROCEDURE

1. Open the bivalve shell.
2. Look for whitish, crescent-shaped marks on the inside of the shell. What do you think made the marks?

EXPLANATION

The crescent-shaped marks are **scars** (marks left where injuries have healed). The scars show where the edges of the bivalve's **mantle** (a fold of the animal's body) was once attached to the shell.

SEASHELL COLORS

Why Are Some Seashells the Colors of a Rainbow Inside?

MATERIALS

abalone shells from the ocean (see drawing)
magnifying lens

Note: If you go into the water to look for shells, ask an adult to watch you.

PROCEDURE

1. Lay the shells so you can see into them.
2. Look into the shells with the magnifying lens.

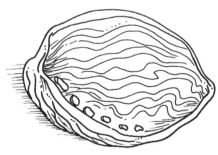

EXPLANATION

The colors you saw inside the shells were caused by light bouncing off the thin layers of shiny material that makes up the lining of the shells. Abalone shells have a variety of rainbowlike colors. Because of these beautiful colors, abalone shells are often used to make combs, buttons, and jewelry.

SUN

The sun is approximately 93 million miles (150 million km) from the earth, yet it is bright enough to light our days. It is also hot enough to burn our skin if we stay outdoors too long in the summer. Without the warmth of the sun, the earth would freeze and become uninhabitable for living creatures.

Find out why our skin tans in the summer, how sunscreen works, how clouds affect the strength of the sun, and more in this section.

SUN AND SKIN

How Does Skin React to Sunlight?

MATERIALS

large mirror

PROCEDURE

1. After you come in from the beach, and while you are changing clothes, look at your body in the mirror.
2. Look to see where your skin is the lightest color and where it is the darkest.

EXPLANATION

The lightest areas of skin, like your buttocks and under your arms, are those that are always covered by your clothes. The darkest areas, like your face and hands, are those that have been exposed to the sun. Some of the sun's rays, called **ultraviolet (UV) rays,** are so strong that they can burn the cells of your skin, causing the top layer to turn red and hurt. This burning is called a **sunburn.** To help protect you from sunburn, your skin cells have a dark-brown **pigment** (color), called **melanin,** that causes your skin to darken instead of burn when exposed to the sun. This darkening is called a **suntan.** People with less melanin have lighter skin, and people with more melanin have darker skin. That's why light-skinned people sunburn more quickly than dark-skinned people.

SCREENING THE SUN

How Does Sunscreen Work?

MATERIALS

photosensitive paper (available at a photography store)
squeeze bottle or squeeze tube of sunscreen, SPF 15 or higher
dark room, such as a closet or a small bathroom without a window
sunlight
watch or timer
paper towel

*Note: The photosensitive paper will be packaged inside a thick,
black, plastic envelope. Don't open the envelope until you
need to use it or the experiment won't work.*

PROCEDURE

1. Take the envelope of photosensitive paper and the sunscreen
   with you into the dark room. Close the door behind you to make the room
   as dark as possible.

2. Open the envelope and slide out a piece of the photosensitive paper. Notice
   that one side of the paper feels slicker than the other. This is the coated
   side.

3. Use the sunscreen to write the first letter of your name on the coated side
   of the paper.

4. Immediately take the paper outside and set it in the sun, coated side up.
   What happens to the paper?

5. After 2 minutes, wipe across the letter with the paper towel. What does the
   paper look like where it was covered with the sunscreen?

EXPLANATION

The photosensitive paper has a special coating that darkens when exposed to
the sun's ultraviolet rays and other forms of light. The paper under the sunscreen stayed lighter because sunscreen has ingredients that block most of the
sun's ultraviolet rays.

83

SUN SPECTACLES

How Do Sunglasses Affect the Eyes?

MATERIALS

dark room
pair of sunglasses

Note: This experiment is best done on bright, sunny days.

PROCEDURE

1. Stay in a dark room for a few minutes (don't wear the sunglasses, but have them with you).
2. Walk outside into the bright sun. What happens to your eyes?

Caution: Never look directly at the sun, even if you are wearing sunglasses.

3. Put the sunglasses on. What happens now?

EXPLANATION

When you walked out into bright sunlight, your eyes felt uncomfortable and may have shed a few tears. When you put on the sunglasses, your eyes felt better because the dark lenses of the glasses stopped some of the sun's **glare** (brightness) from reaching your eyes.

WATER HEAT

How Is Water Heated in Oceans, Rivers, Lakes, and Ponds?

MATERIALS

2 balloons
outdoor cold-water faucet
2 large plastic bowls

2 outdoor thermometers
pin
watch or timer

Note: Handle thermometers carefully, because some are glass and can break easily. If you break a thermometer, don't touch it. Call an adult to do the cleanup.

PROCEDURE

1. Fill both balloons with the same amount of cold water, being careful not to fill them so full that they break.
2. Tie the tops of the balloons.
3. Put each balloon in a bowl.
4. Set one bowl in the sun and the other bowl in the shade. Leave them for at least an hour.
5. Use the pin to break the balloons, letting the water flow into the bowls.
6. Read the thermometers to be sure they register the same temperature. If they have different readings, wait until they read the same. Put a thermometer in each bowl and wait 2 minutes. Which thermometer has the higher reading?

EXPLANATION

The water that was in the sun was warmer than the water that was in the shade. The sun's rays are strong enough to heat water.

GET COOL!

How Does Fanning Cool a Person?

MATERIALS

hot, sunny day
large beach towel or 2 bath towels
water
shady outdoor area

Note: This experiment is best performed on a sunny day, but be sure there is a shady spot.

PROCEDURE

1. On a hot, sunny day, soak the towel(s) in water and wring them out.

Note: If you go into the water to wet the towels, have an adult watch you.

2. Lie down in a shady spot and put the damp towels over your body. What happens?

EXPLANATION

Your body cooled. When your body gets hot, it cools off naturally, by sweating. As the sweat evaporates, your body cools. The water in the wet towel(s) evaporated, cooling your body even more.

COOL COLORS

What Effect Do Colors Have on Cooling?

MATERIALS

white T-shirt
black T-shirt
hot, sunny day
2 outdoor thermometers

*Note: Handle thermometers
carefully, because some
are glass and can break
easily. If you break a thermometer, don't touch it.
Call an adult to do the cleanup.*

Note: This experiment is best performed on a sunny day.

PROCEDURE

1. Read the thermometers to be sure they register the same temperature. If they have different readings, wait until they read the same.
2. Lay the T-shirts next to each other in the sun.
3. Slip a thermometer under each shirt, so the thermometers are completely covered by the shirts.
4. Let the shirts sit in the sun for about 10 minutes.
5. Read the thermometers. Which thermometer recorded the higher temperature?

EXPLANATION

The thermometer under the black shirt had a higher reading than the thermometer under the white shirt. Dark colors absorb (soak up) more heat than light colors. If you wear a black T-shirt on a sunny day, you will feel hotter than if you wear a white one.

87

CLOUD COVER

How Do Clouds Affect the Strength of the Sun?

MATERIALS

2 outdoor thermometers

Note: Handle thermometers carefully, because some are glass and can break easily. If you break a thermometer, don't touch it. Call an adult to do the cleanup.

Note: This experiment is best done on a sunny day, but be sure to have available a shady spot.

PROCEDURE

1. Read the thermometers to be sure they register the same temperature. If they have different readings, wait until they read the same.
2. Place one thermometer in the sun.
3. Place the other thermometer in the shade.
4. After about 10 minutes, read both thermometers. Which one has the higher reading?

EXPLANATION

The thermometer that was in the sun had a higher reading. The shade blocked some of the sun's rays from falling directly on the second thermometer, just as a cloud blocks some of the sun's rays from reaching the surface of the earth. That's why it is usually cooler on a cloudy day than on a sunny day.

SUN'S ANGLE

How Does the Position of the Sun Affect Its Strength?

MATERIALS

sandy beach or a hard, outdoor surface such as a side-
    walk or driveway
measuring tape
friend

*Note: This experiment is best done on a
    sunny day in the early morning or
    late afternoon.*

PROCEDURE

1. Stand in the sun so your
   shadow falls on the sand,
   driveway, or sidewalk.
2. Ask your friend to measure the length of your shadow.
3. Ask your friend to measure your height. Is your shadow longer than your
   height?

EXPLANATION

Your shadow was longer than your height. Early in the morning and late in the
afternoon, the sun is low in the sky and its light comes to you at an angle. (In
the middle of the day, when the sun is directly overhead, there is no angle and
you won't have a shadow.) As the sun's ultraviolet rays pass through the **atmosphere** (the area of gas surrounding the earth), some of them are absorbed.
When the sun is very low in the sky and the sun's angle is the greatest, the
ultraviolet rays have to travel a longer path through the atmosphere, and more
of them are absorbed. That's why sunlight on our skin feels hotter and causes
sunburn faster in the middle of the day than in early morning or late afternoon.

SUN BATH

Why Do Cold-Blooded Animals Lie on Rocks?

MATERIALS

2 identical empty water bottles
aluminum foil
black construction paper
tape
2 bulb-type thermometers
modeling clay
sunny windowsill

PROCEDURE

1. Read the thermometers to be sure they register the same temperature. If they have different readings, wait until they read the same.
2. Cover one bottle with aluminum foil.
3. Cover the other bottle with the black construction paper and tape it in place.
4. Put a thermometer into each bottle so that the bulb is well inside the bottle. Use the clay to seal the top of the bottle around the thermometer.
5. Stand each bottle on the windowsill in the sun.
6. After about 10 minutes, read the thermometers. Which one shows a higher temperature?

EXPLANATION

The bottle with the black paper registered the higher temperature, because the paper absorbed more heat. The aluminum foil on the other bottle reflected much of the heat. Cold-blooded animals, like iguanas, turtles, and other **reptiles** (cold-blooded animals with a backbone and scales), warm themselves on surfaces that absorb heat, such as rocks.

WATER

Water is a colorless liquid that covers most of the earth's surface in the form of oceans, lakes, ponds, and rivers. It is essential to the life of every person, animal, and plant on this planet.

In this section you will see why it is important to protect the earth's water from **pollution** (waste), how water has helped shape our coastlines, and how we use the force of moving water for energy.

DIRTY WATER

Why Should We Protect Our Oceans, Lakes, Ponds, and Rivers from Pollution?

MATERIALS

ocean, lake, or pond beach, or
    riverbank
5 jars
scissors
adult helper

*Note: This experiment is best
performed in sunlight on a
sunny day.*

PROCEDURE

1. Take an adult with you to the beach and collect 5 thrown-away objects, such as a piece of aluminum foil, a plastic spoon, a piece of bread, a balloon, a napkin, and a bottle top.
2. Put each object into a jar. (Some objects, such as paper, foil, or plastic, may have to be cut with the scissors to fit.)
3. Have the adult watch as you wade into the water and fill the jars.
4. Place the jars in sunlight on a windowsill at home.
5. Check the jars in 3 days. What happened to the objects? What might this tell you about objects at oceans, lakes, ponds, and rivers?

EXPLANATION

Some objects, such as paper, may fall apart in water. Pieces of food, such as bread, may be eaten by an animal. Objects made of plastic or metal won't dissolve in water, and a fish or bird may think it is food and eat it. The animal wouldn't be able to digest the object and would die.

RIVER, OCEAN, AND LAKE CREATION

How Were Rivers, Oceans, and Lakes Formed?

MATERIALS

baking dish with straight sides
dry play sand
pitcher
water

PROCEDURE

1. In the center of the baking dish, make a mound of dry sand, higher than the sides of the dish.
2. Fill the pitcher half full with water.
3. Very slowly, pour water on the top of the mound. What happens to the mound?

EXPLANATION

The water trickled down the sides of the mound, carrying away some of the sand in streams. When rain and melting snow run down a mountain, some water is absorbed by plants, soil, and rocks. The water that is not absorbed runs down the mountain, forming ridges, gullies, and hollow spots. The paths the water takes become streams and rivers, which flow into low areas, forming oceans and lakes.

SHORE SCAPE

What Happens When Water Continually Hits the Coastline?

MATERIALS

play sand
yardstick (meterstick)
large, flat area of concrete (driveway
    or sidewalk)
gravel (loose mixture of small stones)
small rocks
large, plastic cup
water

PROCEDURE

1. Use the sand to make about a 3-foot (1-m) arc (curved line) on the concrete.

2. Place the pebbles (small round stones) and rocks at various places around the arc. Leave some areas with sand only.

3. Stand about 3 feet (1 m) away from the center of the arc, and use the cup to toss water on the concrete so the water runs toward the arc, washing against it.

4. Toss water so it washes against different parts of the arc. What happens to the arc?

EXPLANATION

When you tossed the water at the arc, some of the sand washed away, changing the shape of your "coastline." As water pounds against the shore, it gradually wears down the rock. This changes the shape of the coastline, forming new features, such as caves and arches. One coastline might have gentle, sloping beaches, while another might have rocky cliffs and caves.

BOTTLE SINK

Which Sinks More, Water or Sand?

MATERIALS

ocean, lake, or pond with sandy beach
2 identical soda bottles with screw on caps
ruler
funnel
adult helper

PROCEDURE

1. Have the adult watch as you wade into the water and fill one plastic bottle half full with water. Screw on the cap and put the bottle into the water. What happens to the bottle?
2. Take the bottle and add water, about 2 inches (5 cm) at a time, to the bottle, until it sinks.
3. On the beach, use the funnel to fill the second bottle half full with dry sand. Screw on the cap, and have the adult watch as you take the bottle into the water. What happens to the bottle?
4. Keep adding dry sand until the bottle sinks. Does it take more water or more sand to sink a bottle?

EXPLANATION

It took more water. At first, both bottles floated because they contained enough air to keep them buoyant. As you added water and sand to the bottles, it took more water than sand to sink a bottle. Sand weighs about five times more than the same volume of water.

WATER FORCE

Does Moving Water Have Force?

MATERIALS

outside cold-water faucet
plastic toy pinwheel

PROCEDURE

1. Turn on the faucet.
2. Hold the pinwheel under the faucet, so the cold water spins the pinwheel.
3. Turn the water volume a bit higher. What happens to the speed of the pinwheel?

EXPLANATION

When water moves, it has **inertia** (the tendency of a moving object to keep moving). Inertia exerts a force against anything in the water's way. That's why the water turned the pinwheel. The faster the water ran, the faster it pushed the pinwheel. The force of moving water is used to make electricity in power plants. Water that flows over a waterfall or dam turns a **turbine** (a machine much like a bigger, stronger pinwheel). The turbine runs a **generator,** which is a machine that changes motion into electricity.

WATER WALK

How Do Some Animals Walk on Water?

MATERIALS

3-inch (7.5-cm) square of tissue paper
bowl of water
needle
pond, stream, or ocean
field guide to mammals

PROCEDURE

1. Place the tissue paper on the surface of the water in the bowl.
2. Carefully place the needle on top of the tissue paper.
3. Watch the tissue paper and the needle. What eventually happens?
4. At a pond, stream, or ocean, observe some of the animals that stay on the surface of the water. Try to identify these animals by using the field guide.

EXPLANATION

When you placed the needle on the tissue paper, it floated for a while. The paper eventually sank to the bottom, but the needle remained floating. The needle remained floating because it was supported by **surface tension.**

Surface tension is caused by the attraction of water molecules to one another. Some small animals, such as raft spiders and pond skaters, use the surface tension of water. Mosquito larvae hang from the surface of the water, breathing air through **siphons** (tubes that suction). Hydras also use surface tension to hang below the pond surface.

OCEAN HEAT

How Is the Ocean Heated?

MATERIAL

thermometer
ocean, pond, or river
notebook
pencil

*Note: This experiment will take several
minutes two times a year.*

PROCEDURE

1. Hold the thermometer in the water on
    a hot summer day. Be sure to hold the
    top of the thermometer so as not to
    add a false reading.

2. Read the temperature and record it in
    your notebook. Then put your note-
    book away until winter.

3. On a cold winter day, take the tempera-
    ture of the water again and record it in
    your notebook.

4. Compare the difference in temperature.

EXPLANATION

The temperature of the water in the summer was warmer than in the winter.
As ocean water absorbs the sun's **radiation** (light waves sent out), the water
gets warmer. The wind and the waves also add warmth to the water, because
they mix the heat downward. During spring and summer, more heat is
absorbed than is lost, and the temperature of the ocean's surface layer
increases.

NIGHT AND DAY TEMPERATURES

Do Land and Water Temperatures Stay the Same Day and Night?

MATERIALS

thermometer   notebook
ocean   pencil

PROCEDURE

1. Take the temperature of the water during the middle of the day.
2. Now take the temperature of the land.
3. Record the temperatures in your notebook.
4. Take the temperature of the water for 5 minutes during the evening.
5. Take the temperature of the land immediately after taking the water temperature.
6. Compare the day and evening temperatures of the land and the water. How are they different?

EXPLANATION

During the day, the temperature of the land was higher than that of the water. But during the night, the temperature was lower on land than in the water. During the day, warm air rises above the land, and cool air from the sea is drawn underneath the rising warm air. This creates a breeze blowing in from the sea. At night the land cools more quickly as the air begins to sink. The cool air from land pushes out under the warm air over the sea. This creates a breeze blowing out to sea.

UNDER THE ICE

What Happens to Animal and Plant Life When a Pond Freezes?

MATERIALS

hammer
frozen shallow pond
adult helper

Note: Do not go out onto the ice, because it may not support you. Have an adult help you with this experiment.

PROCEDURE

1. Use the hammer to break a chunk of ice in the frozen pond.
2. Look under the ice.

EXPLANATION

When you looked under the ice, you saw the pond was still liquid underneath. The frozen surface is a good insulator for the plant and animal life in the pond. While temperatures above the pond go far below freezing and the winds blow cold air, the pond below the ice is a few degrees above freezing. This allows living things to survive the winter.

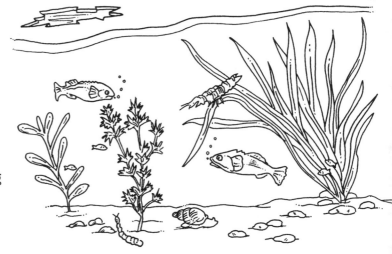

WATER MOVEMENT

A wave is a swell of energy that moves over the surface of a large body of water. Waves can be generated by wind and gravity. A current is the smooth, steady movement of water. Currents are caused by wind, temperature differences, and the interaction of tides.

In this section you can make waves on a dinner plate or in your bathtub, make a whirlpool in a plastic cup, and find out how waves affect the beach.

MAKING WAVES

What Causes Waves?

MATERIALS

dinner plate or bathtub
water
ruler

PROCEDURE

1. Put the dinner plate on a flat surface
   and fill it with water, or fill the bathtub
   to a depth of about 2 inches (5 cm).
2. Blow across the surface of the water.
   What happens to the water?

EXPLANATION

You made waves. Waves are generally
caused by wind. When the wind blows
across the surface of the water, it causes
friction (resistance from the force of one
object sliding against another object). The
friction slows down the speed of the lowest layer of air. This low air layer drags
the top layer of water. Since wind blows in **gusts** (spurts), the drag on the surface is uneven, causing the water to rise and fall in waves. Wave size depends
upon the speed of the wind and how long and how far the wind has been blowing on the water. As the wind blows farther and farther across the ocean or a
large lake, the waves get bigger and farther apart.

WAVE CURLS

Why Do Waves Break As They Reach Shore?

MATERIALS

ocean or lake beach
adult helper

PROCEDURE

1. Sit on the beach and watch the waves. Notice that the waves curl, or break, as they roll in toward the shore.

2. Have the adult watch as you wade into the water so you can more closely observe the waves. Can you see how far from shore they break? Can you guess why they break at that point?

EXPLANATION

As waves reach the shallow water near shore, they break. As the water gets shallower near the beach, the water's movement is slowed by the friction of the water moving against the sand. The waves are slowed and pushed closer together, making them higher. The closer the waves get to the beach, the higher they get, until they curl toward the beach and break. Waves break in water only slightly deeper than their height.

SAND WASH

Do Small and Large Waves Affect the Beach Differently?

MATERIALS

play sand
rectangular cake pan
water

PROCEDURE

1. Build a mound of sand against one end of the pan. Make the mound as high as the pan and about 3 inches (7.5 cm) wide.

2. Gently pour water in the empty area of the cake pan until the pan is half full.

3. At the end of the pan opposite the sand, lightly blow on the water until small waves reach the sand. What happens to the sand?

4. Move closer to the sand area and blow as hard as possible on the water, making bigger waves. What happens to the sand now?

EXPLANATION

When you made small waves, a small amount of sand was washed away. When you made bigger waves, more sand eroded. Waves carry the energy and power of the wind. Gentle waves erode some sand, but large waves erode the sand a great deal more.

WIND WAVES

How Can You Measure the Strength of the Wind to Guess the Size of the Waves?

MATERIALS

scissors
plastic coffee can lid
crepe paper

string
ruler
ocean or lake beach

Note: This experiment is best done on a windy day.

PROCEDURE

1. Use scissors to cut out and remove the inside of the rim of a plastic coffee can lid. Be careful not to cut through the rim, as you want to make a plastic circle.
2. Cut 6–10 strips of crepe paper as long as your arm.
3. Tie the crepe paper strips tightly to the plastic circle. You have made a **windsock** (a device for measuring the strength and direction of wind).
4. Cut a length of string about 2 feet (60 cm) long, and tie each end of the string to the circle, making a hanger for your windsock.
5. On a windy day, hang your windsock where you can see it from the beach. Look at your windsock, then look at the waves. Do this several times. What do you notice?

EXPLANATION

When you looked at the windsock, then at the waves, you could see how much the windsock had to move for the wind to make a certain size wave. After a while, you could look at the windsock and know how big the waves were.

105

UNDERWATER RIPPLES

How Do Snorkelers Find the Beach from Underwater?

MATERIALS

snorkeling gear (optional)
ocean
adult helper

PROCEDURE

1. Have an adult take you snorkeling or just wading so you can look for ripples in the sand on the ocean floor.
2. What do you notice about the ripples?

EXPLANATION

The ripples in the sand are formed by water motion. The ripples are always parallel to the shoreline. Since you know that the ocean becomes shallower toward the beach and that the ripples in the sand are parallel to the beach, then you can find the direction of the beach while snorkeling.

SURFACE MOVEMENT

Does Wind Do More to the Water's Surface Than Make Waves?

MATERIALS

old shirt
rectangular cake pan
water
red, green, or blue food coloring

PROCEDURE

1. Put the old shirt on over your clothes to protect them from the food coloring.
2. Fill the cake pan half full with water and set the pan on a flat surface.
3. Wait until the water in the pan becomes very still, then drop one drop of food coloring onto the water at one end of the pan.
4. Blow on the surface of the water at one corner for several seconds. What happens to the food coloring?

EXPLANATION

When you blew on the water, the surface began to move, carrying the food coloring with it. As you continued blowing, the food coloring moved in a swirling pattern around the pan. This movement is called a **surface current.** Oceans, lakes, and ponds can have surface currents caused by the wind.

COLD CURRENTS

Can Differences in Temperature Move Water?

MATERIALS

old shirt
water
rectangular cake pan
ice cubes
red, green, or blue food coloring
adult helper

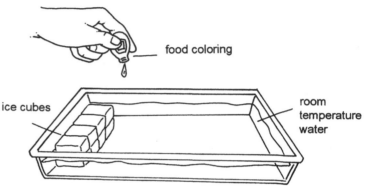

food coloring

ice cubes

room temperature water

PROCEDURE

1. Put the old shirt on over your clothes to protect them from the food coloring.

2. Ask an adult to help you get the water to room temperature by mixing cold and hot water at the tap. Fill the cake pan half full with this water.

3. Set the pan on a flat surface. When the water is very still, stack ice in one end of the pan. Have your helper hold the ice in place.

4. Drop one drop of food coloring onto the water near the ice, and another drop at the opposite end of the pan. After several seconds, what happens to the food coloring?

EXPLANATION

The food coloring moved around the pan in a swirling motion. The ice cooled the water around it. Since cold water is heavier than warm water, the cold water sank, pushing the warmer water out of its way. This created a **cold current.** Oceans, lakes, and ponds can have cold currents. Ocean water travels around the world in currents.

WATER WHIRL

What Happens When Water Spins?

MATERIALS

tall, wide, plastic or paper cup
water
small piece of sponge
craft stick

PROCEDURE

1. Fill the cup with water.
2. Drop the small piece of sponge on the water.
3. Use the craft stick to stir the water very fast in one direction. What happens to the water?
4. What happens to the sponge as you stir?

EXPLANATION

When you stirred the water, it swirled around. The water moved up higher on the sides of the cup and dropped lower in the center of the cup, creating a current called a **whirlpool.** The sponge was moved to the center of the whirlpool and pulled downward. Whirlpools can form in lakes and rivers where two currents meet. In the ocean, whirlpools can be created by tides interacting.

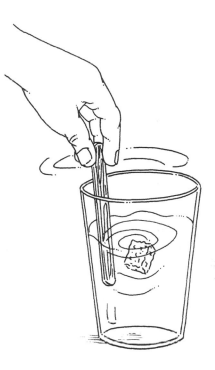

RIVER FLOW

How Fast Does a River Flow?

MATERIALS

tape measure   stopwatch
riverbank   butterfly net
rocks   adult helper
orange

PROCEDURE

30 feet

1. Measure 30 feet (10 m) along the sides of a riverbank.

2. Place some rocks or another marker at each end of the measurement.

3. Stand at one end of the measured area and have an adult stand downstream. Drop the orange in the water and start the stopwatch.

4. Time how long it takes for the orange to get to the end of the measured area downstream.

5. Retrieve the orange with the butterfly net.

EXPLANATION

Rivers flow about 2 miles per hour (3 km/h). That means it should take about 12 seconds for your orange to go from one marker to the next. In a fast stream the orange will go faster, while in a slower stream the orange might take about 44 seconds to get from one marker to the next.

RIVER FORMATION

How Do Rivers Form?

MATERIALS

water
pail
sandpile or sandy area

PROCEDURE

1. Form an area of sloping sand.
2. Fill the pail with water.
3. Pour some water at the top of the slope until the water begins to run.
4. From a different point on top of the slope, pour some more water until it begins to run.
5. Repeat step 3 several times from different points. Where does the water end up?

EXPLANATION

When you poured water at the top of the sloping sand, it randomly ran down to a stopping point. Each time you poured water from a different place, it ended up at the same stopping point and met the stream previously poured. A river is usually formed when many small streams meet. A very tiny stream is called a rivulet. Rivulets usually flow into a larger stream. The stream moves on to meet a larger river. Then the river flows on to the ocean.

WATER MOTION

Are Water Motion and Wave Motion the Same?

MATERIALS

bathtub
water
tissue paper about 2½ inches (6 cm) square
ruler

PROCEDURE

1. Fill the bathtub with water.
2. Blow on the water at one end of the tub to produce miniature waves.
3. Place the piece of tissue paper in the water.
4. Blow on the water about 6 inches (15 cm) away from the tissue paper. What happens to the tissue paper?

EXPLANATION

When you blew on the water, you caused the water to make waves. When you placed the tissue paper in the water and blew, the paper bobbed up and down and back and forth. But it did not move to the end of the tub with the wave. The forward motion of the water seemed to be moving, but the water did not move. The wave pattern moved, but not the water.

Marine and Wildlife Organizations

Write to these organizations for more information on marine life:

American Crustacean Society
P.O. Box 4416
San Pedro, CA 90731
310-548-6279

Center for Marine Conservation
1725 DeSales Street, NW
Washington, DC 20036
202-429-5600

Cousteau Society
870 Greenbrier Circle
Chesapeake, VA 23320
804-523-9335

Crustacean Society International
21 Laurel Hill Road
Ridgefield, CT 06877
203-544-8617

Greenpeace U.S.A.
1436 U Street, NW
Washington, DC 20009
202-462-1177

Izaak Walton League of America
1401 Wilson Boulevard, Level B
Arlington, VA 22209
703-528-1818

National Audubon Society
555 Audubon Street
Sacramento, CA 85825
916-481-5332

National Conservatory
625 North Adams Street
Tallahassee, FL 32310
904-222-0199

National Geographic Society
Educational Services Department
1145 17th Street, NW
Washington, DC 20036
800-647-5463

National Wildlife Federation
1400 16th Street, NW
Washington, DC 20036
202-797-6800

Oregon Coast Aquarium
2820 SE Ferry Slip Road
Newport, OR 97365-9907
541-867-3474

Padilla Bay National Estuarine Research Center
1043 Bayview Edison Road
Mount Vernon, WA 98273
360-428-1558

Glossary

absorb: to soak up.

acid: a substance that can react with and dissolve certain metals.

adhesion: the attraction between two substances.

agar: a substance prepared from red algae that is used as a food additive.

algae: water plants that contain chlorophyll and make their own food.

amphibians: animals that live underwater as babies, then breathe air as adults.

aquatic: of the water.

area: surface space.

atmosphere: the gas mass surrounding the earth.

barnacles: small shellfish that attach themselves to objects in seawater.

barrier reef: an offshore coral reef that is parallel to the beach.

bivalve: a mollusk, such as an oyster or clam, that forms a shell with two halves.

bladder: an inflatable sac.

bladder wrack: a seaweed with forked, brownish-green fronds. Also called **rockweed.**

blowhole: a slit for breathing located on top of a whale's head.

buoyancy: tendency to float.

calcium carbonate: white crystal-like compound used by certain sea animals to build shells.

carbon dioxide: a gas breathed out by people and animals.

casts: small, cone-shaped piles of sand thrown out as waste.

cell: the basic unit of all plants and animals.

cohesion: the attraction of like molecules to each other.

cold-blooded: having a body temperature that adapts to the environment.

cold current: movement of water due to differences in temperature.

compound: a substance formed by the combination of two substances.

compress: to squeeze together.

conch: a shellfish with a large spiral-shaped shell.

contract: to decrease in volume, scope, or size.

crustaceans: a group of animals that have bodies covered with shells made of segments.

crystals: regularly shaped pieces into which many substances are formed when they become solids.

debris: waste.

deltas: areas at the mouths of rivers formed by deposits of sediments carried downstream.

density: weight compared to volume.

digest: to break down food for use by the body.

displace: to push aside.

dissolve: to mix completely with a liquid.

distort: to cause an object to look like it has a different shape than it really does.

dormant: resting.

echo: a reflection of sound.

echolocation: bouncing sound off an object to determine its location.

element: a substance that can't be broken down by chemical action.

erosion: the wearing away of rock and soil by natural forces, such as water, wind, and gravity.

estuary: ocean inlet.

ethology: study of animal behavior

evaporate: to change to a gas.

expand: to increase in volume, scope, or size.

extract: to take from.

filter: to purify a liquid by passing it through porous matter to remove suspended substances.

flatfish: a certain group of fish with bodies that are flat.

foliage: leaves.

friction: resistance from the force of one object moving against another object.

fronds: the leaflike structures of seaweed and certain other plants.

garnet: a common, crystal-like, red mineral found in some rocks.

gastropod: a mollusk that grows in a shell, such as a snail.

gel: jellylike substance.

generator: a machine that turns motion into electricity.

gills: the breathing organs of a fish.

glare: brightness.

granite: a very hard, igneous rock.

gravitational attraction: the pull of gravity.

gravity: the force that pulls everything toward the center of the earth.

gust: spurt.

guyot: a seamount that has risen to the surface of the ocean and formed an island.

hermit crab: a small crab with an unprotected abdomen that lives in shells formed by other animals, especially snails.

hibernate: to rest.

holdfast: a rootlike structure of seaweed that secretes a sticky substance that bonds with rocks and shells.

hornblende: a green, bluish-green, or black mineral found in igneous rock.

hydrometer: an instrument that measures the density of liquids.

igneous rock: rock formed by great heat under the earth's surface.

inertia: the tendency of a moving object to keep moving.

insulate: to prevent passage of heat, electricity, or sound.

limpet: a gastropod with a tent-shaped shell.

locomotion: movement.

low tide: when the water is lowest on the beach.

lugworms: sea worms that have many bristles on the sides of their body sections.

mammals: warm-blooded animals that have backbones, and the females of which give birth to live young and feed them with milk from mammary glands.

mantle: a folded-over part of a bivalve's body.

melanin: a pigment in skin that causes it to darken when exposed to sunlight.

metamorphic rock: rock formed by heat or pressure.

meteorite: a rock from space that landed on Earth.

mica: a flaky mineral found in some rocks.

micrometeorite: a dustlike particle from space.

mineral: element or compound with a crystal-like structure.

molecule: the smallest part of an element.

mollusk: a soft-bodied ocean animal that grows a shell for protection.

Newton's third law of motion: a law of physics which states that for every action there is an equal but opposite reaction.

nymphs: young insects.

oil slick: an area of oil floating on water.

olivine: a green, crystal mineral found in certain rocks.

operculum: the flap of a fish gill.

oxygen: a colorless, tasteless, odorless gas.

oystercatcher: a chicken-size beach bird with a blackish-brown-and-white body, long red bill, and pink feet.

perennial: growing back each year.

pigment: color.

pincers: large claws.

pollution: waste products in air, water, or land.

predator: an animal that kills another for food.

propulsion: a force that pushes.

quartz: a hard mineral found in granite rock.

quartzite: a rock formed by the crystallizing of sandstone.

radiation: light waves sent out.

red algae: a type of seaweed.

reflect: to bounce off a surface, as light bounces off a mirror.

repel: to push away.

reptile: a cold-blooded animal with a backbone and scales.

residue: the remainder of a substance after removal of a part.

rockweed: see **bladder wrack.**

sandbar: a long, underwater ridge of sand and gravel near the shore.

scales: thin, flexible structures that overlap to form a protective covering on fish.

scar: a mark left where an injury has healed.

sea lettuce: a bright green seaweed that resembles salad lettuce.

seamount: a volcano that has risen from the ocean floor, but has not reached the surface.

sedges: perennial herbs found in wetlands.

sedimentary rock: rock formed by matter pressing together.

sediments: matter that settles.

segments: sections.

siphon: a tube that suctions.

sodium chloride: the chemical name for salt.

sound waves: vibrations of air caused by a moving object.

spawn: the eggs of aquatic animals, such as mollusks and fish.

spines: sharp, stiff projections.

spire: the pointy spiral of a gastropod shell.

sunburn: a reddening of the skin caused by the ultraviolet rays of the sun.

suntan: a reaction of the skin to sunlight that causes the skin to darken.

surface current: movement of surface water in one direction.

surface tension: attraction of water molecules to one another.

tide pool: low area of ocean beach that traps water when the tide goes out.

tides: changes in the water level caused by changes in the gravitational attraction of the earth and moon.

transform: to change.

translucent: able to allow some light to pass through.

turbine: a machine that spins, much like a pinwheel, from the force of water.

ultraviolet (UV) rays: certain sun rays that can burn human skin.

vegetation: plants.

vertebrate: an animal with a backbone.

volume: the amount of space inside that has length, width, and height.

warm-blooded: having a body temperature that is regulated to stay the same.

water vapor: water in gas form.

webbed feet: feet on which the toes are connected to each other by a section of skin.

wetland: land soaked with water.

whirlpool: a spiral current formed where two currents meet.

windsock: a device that indicates the strength and direction of wind.

INDEX

Made in the USA
Middletown, DE
28 April 2015